ALSO BY KATY WAREHAM MORRIS

Making Tracks	(V. Press, 2020)
Cutting the Green Ribbon	(Hesterglock Press, 2018)
Inheritance, with Ruth Stacey	(Mother's Milk Books, 2016)

VIOLET EXISTENCE

Katy Wareham Morris

ISBN: 978-1-915079-22-0

Cover designed by Aaron Kent

Edited and typeset by Aaron Kent

Broken Sleep Books Ltd
Rhydwen,
Talgarreg,
SA44 4HB
Wales

Contents

Violet Existence

Katy Wareham Morris

Labour

I

She lay on stiff white linen, sleeping:
head lolled back, palms loose
in surrender. Kept warm for
days by the pastel-dotted nightie,
buttons now undone. All that
potential. When she stirs, everyone is looking,
even her dad. She is jammed
behind her own eyes, jailbird
of a romantic myth shown in photos
that never looked like this.
                              Her body
backfires into flamenco, she doesn't know
flamenco.

II

by day ~~four~~ five (?)
                she was
rammed into another room

they tried to get a line in whilst dancing   *why?*
they tried to push down with a mask   *why?*

bright light stung the back of her eyes
        hormone drip
        gas and air

        drip   breathe
        drip   drip   breathe
        breathe   *breathe*

                                                        what
                        came first?
                                                what's
                        bleeping?

~~something forced~~ her eyes closed
                                                        how

much time?

before she sat up static-charged
        green   *(no!)*
        black
        sick shooting
flooding the linens
turning pastels to mud.

III

no one moves
no one   ~~hears her~~

as if hypnotised

she

        lifts and

             twirls

               lifts and

                      twirls

she is caught on a riptide
         capsizing
         sliding

head lolled back
palms l o o s e

If only I could hold them for a thousand years

I would let the beetles crawl in my open palms
as if wandering through bowed lotus petals,
porcelain wings clapping - *we are not afraid.*
I would let their storm-slicked shells peck at my porous skin,
enchanted by the scent of pomegranate and honey –
I'm sorry evaporates from each leaf finger,
encouraging them to dance, continue searching
for one speck of pollen.
If only their eyes remained distracted, they could
keep filling their mottled bellies and I would
let my body turn to stone.

Mother said

Be brave be kind
Use your listening ears
Snooze   Grow

There'll be times

                                       B r e a t h e
                                       Salute the sun

                      how?

Say please say thank you
Sing many many songs
Chase   Play

They won't bite

                                  Close your eyes
                                  The mind swims

                   where?

Don't fight calm down
Use your gentle hands / voices
Plait   Weave

If they don't want

                              Rhythms will take you
                                     peace

                   why?

Speak up speak out
Look both ways
Read   Draw

Sorry means

                              Heart B E A T S
                              Time waits

will it?

Make friends break friends
Find the up and up
Dig   Dream

It's always the   Listen to rain
                                                   B a t h e

is it?

You will you can
Get back up again
Lose   Be bold

Love   *pitchy pitchy*
                                chappy chappy
                        rrrammm rrrrammm rrrammm

I'm OK, Now

How old was I when the reams of green came home? I can't find the colour – lime. Maybe chartreuse, but no kid knows that word. Fuck, I don't know that word. It was stripy with holes down the sides. In my mind they're the holes punched in the kids' copy of *The Hungry Caterpillar*. Strange isn't it? Where it takes you.

If we'd been gentle, we could've torn along the perforations, separated the holes from the banded block. We didn't give a gentle fuck. That hasn't changed. The kids' fucked my favourite work pen yesterday. *I told you to use gentle hands.* Stacked, until you lifted the top sheet. An arm's length revealed a vertical accordion, pealing paper of coded Courier: your programme.

We turned it around: skies, clouds, flowers, potatoes as people, sometimes rainbows. I began writing along the lines. Why was it green? Why was it stripy? *Be grateful you've got paper.* Even then I thought too much.

One time you brought home a fresh stack and you sat next to us at the table. I'd never seen you doodle. We sat together, stuck between the lines. Not long after, you tossed your stubby yellow pencil and sighed. Maybe you weren't a fan of green stripes either? More skies, clouds, flowers, potato people and rainbows.

Enter the Father from stage left, backlit from the window – glowing. A thick nightmare descends, thunders. The stripy accordion is silent. The ensemble is silent. Fuck.

Being Shadow

For my brother

On the off-chance that you might let me in,
I agree to sit compliantly at the head of your bed,
agree to have the dodgy controller, hope
to play our relationship on fast forward for a while.
Parkouring to an arcade soap opera theme, you batter
the buttons. I feel ringing in my ears. When my spin jump
doesn't make it, you turn
to look at me
for the first time

you're straight into rolling attack but
I am sat behind, remember? Your aura -
I would sacrifice everything. Maybe

we hit chaos control, suddenly you are
sat between my two kids showing them
how to spin jump, quick-step rivals.
They may be the wind, but
we are closer than you know.

Trouble in Paradise

Thank you for asking how I was over lunch. Did you notice I was quiet because I didn't understand the references to tragedy and why the Greeks were much more civilised? I was thinking about last night's tragedy - that lovely girl from *Love Island* was made to think her lovely boyfriend was with another girl in a cruel twist from the mischievous producers and she was distraught. Full on red-in-the-face blarting. Tonight I shall find out whether their relationship passes the test. Everyone's talking about it, and I don't even know how or why, but you lot all chipped in about mothers killing and eating their babbies, ladling heads out of pastry lids and how it all happens off-stage for the Greeks. I looked down and ate my home-made sandwich in a fashion: both hands secured the bread, left the crisp packet unrustled, salt in the corner. I didn't drink from the bottle, remembering to sip slowly, carefully from a barely filled cup. Tomorrow, I shall not discuss my thoughts on the manipulation of classical tragic tropes in reality television by way of affecting an apathetic millennial audience. I've heard it all before.

When I feel anxious, I listen for the wind

Murmurs froth through
the broken seal   I stand
by the kettle   hear rumblings
in my stomach   *if only*
licks

the left side of my face
whip away   bend double
flay forward   cheerleading pom poms
earth me   then   twist away
interrupted by the clock   I try to
be still   rooted   unfastening   slack
lack of intention

yet knitted   knotted
to the frame   *come again*

Immediately after the terrorists set off their bombs

When you were small you would press your toes into the sand,
wiggle them, enjoy the grittiness. You would race to scoop it up,
falling away through all your fingers, heap it up onto your bodies,
press your downy legs together, pack it down tight till there were
no more legs, only the torsos of gods emerging from
a thousand years of see-sawing sea on rocks.
Then, you'd kick up those legs, whose I couldn't tell,
tentacles flailing, shaking off tails, leaving fine sand-papery skin.
How to save that skin now?

I will lie you both down softly in the tall grasses that speak
like waves. I will press your downy legs together, clasp your hands
so you know you're safe, you have each other. And then I will
pluck the strands of green that remind me of rain, I will pluck
the foxgloves, the buttercups, wild geranium, even dandelions.
I will pull together this posy, scatter it over your cold, church-like
tombs. I will dress you, bathe you in apple green dewy leaves.
I will let little crawlies find the nooks and crannies of you both,
make friends with your pixie nose, your dimpled chin. When
only your heads remain, I will crown you both with daisies,
close your eyes, kiss you in turn, then let the blossom-filled
branches touch your faces, hide them. With time you will sink
into the soil, soothed by its silt. It will pack down tight till
there are no more legs, not even the torsos of gods. Then,
I will give in to the sun, let the blood-red sky eat me.

When summer wouldn't stop, I remembered

Someone once told me
the globe was gutted & breaking
& I thought that was scary:
a cruel destiny.
Somehow though, it was beautiful
because someone loved enough
to notice.

What was I supposed to do
when the ground went hard, cracked,
lost its colour? Lost its lives?
I couldn't stop a fate
from coming. I didn't have
the power
to command the clouds &
stem the bleeding.

I tried to rustle up the atmosphere,
but then
            the sand came &

violet candyfloss marshmallows.

After the strangled screeches we thought were thunder, a reverie

Shushing dust settles into a crap-clouded dark
        you heard white pulsing before it leapt in the air

after   we shelter in soft shadows
listening for your hollowing clear

billy owl jenny owl willow owl gilly white barn owl

my ears dissolve in wanderer's delight
        sedated by your still speculation

silhouettes reveal what day conceals
        bodies exploded   fierce operas of light

monkey-faced silver owl steeple owl billy wise barn owl

huddled in groves once green
        fireworks fade and sleep

dappled with whispers of your heart-shaped face
        sunburnt hills cease wailing

dobby owl hobby owl hobgoblin ghost owl barn owl

Nothing
                cries
when the spirit feels

golden owl banshee church owl death owl barn owl

bright confusions of man's loud singing
      bramble-rose
              cowslip
                     foxglove
torn-up forage in teeth

ripped up babbies
      eyes pulled through

morning chiaroscuro
      seeking
      circling
too high for syllables to speak
                                 billy owl jenny
owl willow owl gilly white barn owl
                  monkey-faced silver owl steeple owl billy wise barn owl
                              dobby owl hobby
owl hobgoblin ghost owl barn owl
                golden owl banshee church owl death owl
barn owl
tyto alba
      tyto alba
         tyto alba

After the Horses

Seaswindsmeadowsweathers
swallowed by an unknown jaw
shrieking oratorio   bluegreengreyhalo
fountains of blackblackblack
acidrainsrainsrains dissolved
every frost that there ever was
ever had been   effervescing
in torch-light beam-light
  heatheatheat of new suns
guzzling every squalling
billowblastblowblowblow
of shredded shrapnel confetti
  catching lighteningstrobe sky like
new stars   illuminating heaving viscosities
of smogssmokesvapours   devoured us
in front of the fluff that had
held us in suspended stasis

through bite marks   wrenched-up-roots
mangled metals swirled in bile   reeked
around shadows thrown against boiling moons
  we dumb-struck crawled with burningbloods
cancercancercancer diffusing
into shaved skiescreaturespastures
  grasses grabbed wild lifedeath
already melted crittersplinters
teased voraciously   making us
sleepy   eerie entertainment gurgled
in our ears   we needed that
we had forgotten how to believe our eyes

Posthuman Coloratura

We seemed to soar for days
before crashing   *buried*
        we daren't look up

grey clay stuck to skin
sieving through fatbergs   *clawing*
        at foam   pearly wires

under shattered pinata
clouds sung   *neon*
        mysteries repeated

tempered flesh
roosting   heaps of   p a p e r   d o l l s

Diary / Faces

Promises / Gappy toothy grin

I'm a princess. This dress swishes - pretend I'm dancing, there's no music. Sometimes I get hot and scratchy. I only half skip cos I know they're watching. They never dance. I stand still when they tell me, when they take my photo. They say I'm tall. I'm a good girl. I really want a dolly. I could talk to it and stop pulling my hair. They say if I'm good, the birthday fairies will come. I keep waiting. I promise to be -

Before (and after, if they could) / Resting bitch

Your skirt looks nice you say. You're really stunning, such long legs. My skin turns to chopped ham and cold custard. Their lips barely move upwards and if it wasn't for the clear throat and guttural tone, you'd think they were nervous. Hollow. I don't think they know that tights give you thrush. Don't you get cold? Don't your shoes rub? They wring their clasped hands as if feeling my pain already. Maybe pleading. Womanhood is risky: blisters or crusty cunts. Maybe frostbite. Have you had your hair done you say? Very dramatic. I wish I could be as brave.

What if? / Bags

Having shelled two healthy children – I'm lucky. Should I tell her that you only bake with fresh eggs? That you bite your lip, but don't always close your eyes? Will his father let him know? I keep this house as their incubator. Tonight, I will thank Jamie Oliver for the inspiration that produced another clean, colourful, med-inspired family meal that everyone will eat with enthusiasm. Without their warmth, there would be time for boredom. And thinking.

Nothing happened / Come to bed

A whore is a whore. (Un)dressed in the standard issue (ripped) fishnets and basque. Not even hiding behind those - Asking for it. Desperate. It is a satisfactory acceptance. A reason to be. You fuck the pain away. Afterwards, you shed that skin and develop new scales. Markings on the skin titillate. Their imprint. I imagine grass. Tall grass swaying sideways, like a slinky falling down stairs.

~~An Advert~~ For This Body

I am **able**,
competent.
                                                  A doing-person.
                                    Busy, always busy. I don't
                                                              quit
                                              (I did but I don't now).
                                    I'm a perfectionist. I'm
                                                        toxic.
                                    People say I'm hard on myself. People
                                    ask for more /
                                    tell me what they think /
                                    say I'm strong / brave /
                        w a s t i n g   a w a y / / / / /
                                    never looked better / high maintenance /
                                    controlling / confident / assertive /
                                              I'm an empath. I ***can***not be

                  worn down / worn ~~out~~. I can't
                                                              quit.
                              I've   l o s t   ~~weight~~
                                                  surviving
                  even though
                                    I'm thinner, I'm still
                                                              ~~fat~~.
                                    They were shuck from me.
                                                  I'm husk.
                  Frozen | a b a n d o n e d
                                                  by motherhood.
                                                        No one
                                                  tells you that
                        People ~~notice~~   when you
                        become soft   on the
                              outside.

Maybe
I'm ~~attractive~~.

I am **able**,
competent.

I turn up, galvanise / surprise.
It makes you sssssexy. No one knows

I want to be

~~thin~~.
I need to feel pressure otherwise I'm
~~disappearing~~
annoying ~~myself~~.
I smile, say ~~sorry~~ too much. I like my own company.

I'm

tired............

~~fat~~   ~~struggling~~

–

I am **able**,
competent.

s t i l l
I'm |

But I am *sick*.
Can you see that now? I can't

~~quit~~.

Curry Night

Could you lemme know if it's ok to talk about bein' a mother an' *Masterchef*, which I love? It's gone 7pm and me brain heaves out bodies without organs and transhuman digital futures like…

I eat with me fingers usin' roti for cutlery, like me mates taught me. Order sides with me main 'cos that's how we do it. I'm still wearin' me work clothes which was silly 'cos me top is white an' I eat whilst I'm talkin', prone to spillin'.

Did you take a deep breath 'cos I didn't order off the menu? I'd recommend it for you but you're safe: masala / korma / jalfrezi / bhuna. I don't drink 'cos I've got Crohn's (I don't drink 'cos I over-share).

I won't come for a drink 'cos I don't drink. I'll drive home, kiss me kids, cuddle me dog, sit on me sofa, watch *Masterchef*, which I love. I'll say thanks to the wait staff. I'll offer the tip.

In Portrait Mode: Studio Finish

I took pictures because
               something to share   I wanted to be
                                                visible ~~again~~

I need to be
              ~~liked again~~

F R O N T   D O O R
I
                                    washed in white

M I R R O R E D   W A L L

Beautiful
               like this   Zoom-focussed lines / wrinkles
s
o
f
t
e
n

2 images
<u>hair up</u>   <u>hair down</u>
orderly   uncertain
function   freedom
greys / roots   kinks / curls
responsibility   youth
                        cheekbones
                            so gorg
                      strong jaw
                      family nose
                          stunning

I   s   m   i   l   e   d

with TEETH   *unreal*

digging into lines

        b   l   e   n   d

           like magic

hidden ~~darkness~~

       mellow flaxen shades

~~sickness~~

          love it!

I am **peach**

      soft / full / ruddy

           for action

    p 0 i 1 x 0 e 1 1 0 a 1 t 0 e 1 d

struggle to

     time / tools / methods to practice

77 likes   gawking

         balking

Role Play

I had on a couple of occasions indulged you in conversations about your art but today you were talking about your toil, your commute and the all-too-needy students who had been overly-mothered. They sit in your time like shiny pebbles damming the sea, you are the unwilling seaweed flung against their face. You think of them as the elves and you Father Christmas, but they are the kiddies desperate to sit on your lap and prove they've been good. Then you said it and I didn't know if I'd heard it, but you had. You wondered whether you had a case for pay discrimination, you were in the union. You thought it was a good sound case actually. Most men in your position with your experience get offered the senior post straight away and you wondered why you were stuck at the top of one scale, unable to make it over the stile. There was no helping hand to help heave you over and now you knew how it felt to be one of *those women*. Then you said, look at this video. I didn't know it would be you stroking your nipples. I realised then that you too were a kid sat on the lap of an older guy who is dressed up and muffling, pretending to know you and pretending to care. Was it more socially awkward to watch you tease your nipples to the sound of bad music or, to stand next to one another both heads turned down both muffling? Hoping to be the good kiddies. You didn't know how to audibly exhale through flared nostrils either. I looked at you then, sat in half hero, half lotus pose and I thought what a fragile little Barbie eunuch you are.

I have forgotten (it's not about me)

The smell   of the world when   thick
with ice and   light.
It pinched   my lungs   washed my
face.   The shape
of the world when   sandwiched between   blues /
reds   stamps birds   in black.   It lashed
        me to space   fixed
me below.   The softness   of
the world when   ribboned with dandelions and daisies.
            Dirt   stuck to my gums
        as I   .
rol
  1
   1
    1
     1
      1
       1
        1
         1
          1
           1
            1
             1
              1
               1
                1
                 1
                  1
                   1
                    1
                     1
                      1
                       1
                        1
                         1
                          1
                           1
                    ed

Summer evening, before

I guess I hadn't noticed that the bees had stopped. Nature is noisy, so I don't know how I missed it. No one thought the flowers would die. Even when the heat came, there was no colour. There was no colour that summer. How did I miss it? There was no pure blue sky; no monstrous rhododendrons, azalea, clematis, buddleia, freesia. Not a single buttercup to hold to see if she liked butter; not a single daisy to make a chain for her bony wrist. There, I've said all the flowers I know.

Did the grass smell? I did not get the itch and it didn't need cutting. It was golden but without the energy and relativity to produce glow; no twilight, no twinkle. A miniature harvest of straw blades stood there, crispy under foot yet without sound. There were no noisy bees, so there could be no crunchy lawns?

The sky was a padded duvet pressing down on us, holding us tight to stop our reach, our spread, our busy virility. If it couldn't breathe, neither could we. Made of charged nylon, you couldn't look up because you might be zapped by the dark light that slinked between the fleece. The clouds didn't clear and the red, purple, pink, orange sky never came at night. No shepherd's delight, no warning.

One day it rained. Was it about 6.30pm? Everyone – everything – else had gone. I remember a sound on my roof; nature is noisy. Perhaps this cleared the clouds. I didn't stop. How do I know this was rain? Hundreds of brushstrokes licking the taut surface of a bass drum; stippling the skin of an over-blown balloon.

I saw dust on the windowsill, the colour of Barcelona like she had crushed up her chalks again, leaving the crumbs to show me how to find her and choosing the colour of blood oranges and Emperor's Silk. There was colour. There was warning? I rubbed it between my fingers. If I look closely, the colour remains in the swirling ridges of my fingerprint.

Dust covered the ground outside like when snow falls as flurries and then becomes bigger, thicker. The bigger ones stick because of the tiny, almost unnoticeable flurries beneath. It lay on the ground like the first falls of burnt snow; the air full of dust and the clouds that pressed. This was the only rain there was. The only rain there could be.

I drove through pink smoke; pomegranate dust whipped into the air against the blanked-out canvas of the duvet sky. There was colour. It could've been one of her drawings, candyfloss plumes filled the page: inside the clouds is where she said the magic happened. Was this magic?

When I close my eyes the picture blurs and I can no longer see her face, her eyes, her perfect bow-shaped lip, that prominent M-shaped bow, and the delicately upturned nose - the family nose, my nose. I stroked my nose then, and now: pretend it's hers.

Everything was bathed in dust like I'd blown my blusher compact and all of the tiny fragments of cerise shimmer had landed on crisp white fittings and furnishings, hot splatters against plastics like spray paint. Was it powder or grit? I did not feel a sense of dramatic foreboding; there was no warning, remember.

I did not think of flamingos French-rose fuchsia lavender watermelon salmon peonies peaches poppies strawberries raspberry-honeysuckle geraniums cherries coral carnations cherry-blossom conch shell quartz amethyst sun-kissed-dusky wood boysenberry-blood. What about her blushing ballet slippers?

I opened the door to the lounge; the curtains weren't quite meeting. A milky way of dust. I had forgotten the bees, the flowers, the grass, the rain. It did not feel like home or childhood.

Then she was there

waving in violet winds
        tall
aubergine heather mulberry orchid
bending
        stretching
                saluting the sun

small buds turning
                    twirling
blushing bells ringing
                    flouncing skirts
                                        teasing
acid yellow
            purple dapples
                                periwinkle pockets
ready to jig
            elf-like kicking
                                upwards on heels
apple green neon whiff

Foxglove riff:
for now
namaste

They are the World.

Acknowledgements

I would like to thank Aaron Kent from Broken Sleep Books for giving me the opportunity to publish these poems. I have especially appreciated Aaron's enthusiasm for my work. These poems examine my relationship with my body, my family, my work and the world. They explore the many and varied ways I am challenged by these experiences; for these reasons, the poems themselves can be challenging. They represent the pervasive nature of my Imposter Syndrome: an imposter in my own body, family, work and the world. And of course, in the 'world of poetry'. This is why Aaron's support and encouragement means so much. Thank you, Aaron for caring about these poems and by default caring about me.

Thanks also to John McCullough who originally judged these poems and awarded them the Runner-up position in the Prole Pamphlet Competition (thanks also to Brett Evans and Phil Robertson from Prole of course, for running the competition) in 2020. I am blown away by John's apposite and munificent endorsement, capturing almost precisely what I had hoped to achieve with these poems. Again, his enthusiasm and support of my writing is hugely appreciated. I have long been a fan of John's work: his writing, his experience, his generosity of spirit also helps me believe that 'real' people can make it poetry.

Thanks should also go to Pascale Petit and Andrew McMillan whose writing workshops helped inspire some of these poems and, whose editing tutorials helped tighten others. It was a huge honour to be tutored by them both whilst on an Arvon Writing Retreat at The Hurst in the summer of 2019.

I would also like to thank my friend and colleague at the University of Worcester, Dr Sharon Young for introducing me to the poetry of Anne Finch; *A Nocturnal Reverie* soon became a favourite and was in the forefront of my mind whilst writing, *After the strangled screeches were thought were thunder, a reverie.* I thank Sharon for her insight and expertise at that time, and now, but especially for the chats (and pep talks!) over coffee which keep me believing that I can be a poet and an academic.

I would like to give space to Sharon and my other female colleagues at the University of Worcester: Dr Lucy Arnold, Holly Barnes-Bennetts, Prof. Nicoleta Cinpoeş, Jenny Lewin-Jones, Dr Barbara Mitra, Ruth Stacey and Dr Whitney Standlee. It's not easy being a female academic. I appreciate you all: your innovative research, your commitment to your teaching, your support of students and your unwavering support of me.

I thank the friends who listen to me ramble about my research and writing. Who listen to the long-winded response to a simple, 'How are you?'. Who tell me that I'm not such a bad mother after all. Thank you: Claire Bou Aziz, Carly Bradshaw, Nina Chauhan-Lall, Shanty Devi, Claire Dickenson and Rachel Georgiou.

I must thank my parents: they continue to give me everything. I would be nothing without them. They inspire me and my children. I thank my brother for being himself, always.

Thank you of course to my husband, Simon for continuing this struggle we call marriage, parenthood, life. Our children are mesmerising: testament of everything that is possible when we're together.

Rosalind and Alastair – you are everything and always will be. Remember: be kind; be brave.

Notes

Summer evening, before first appeared in the online magazine, *Mooky Chick* (selected by Charley Barnes, March 2020).

Being Shadow first appeared in *Hit Points: An Anthology of Video Game Poetry* (Eds. Aaron Kent and Matthew Haigh, Broken Sleep Books, 2021).

When summer wouldn't stop, I remembered is inspired by the poem, *Song for Baby-O, Unborn* by Diane di Prima.

After the Horses is inspired by the poem, *The Horses* by Edwin Muir.

LAY OUT YOUR UNREST